PRAYING FOR ...

containing

Praying for Others

&

Praying for Yourself

by

Katherine Hilditch

This book contains two booklets from Life in Jesus:

1. Praying for Others – page 1

2. Praying for Yourself – page 13

Being Born-Again – page 25

Praying for Others
Copyright © 2014 Katherine Hilditch
All rights reserved.

Praying for Yourself
Copyright © 2014 Katherine Hilditch
All rights reserved.

Unless otherwise indicated
all Scripture quotations are taken from
the World English Bible British Edition (WEBBE)

(Any words in brackets are not in the original text
but are included to help understanding)

1

Praying for Others

Are you sometimes unsure how to pray for someone? Or do you feel your prayers for others aren't being answered? Are you frustrated that someone you love is struggling and your prayers don't seem to be making any difference?

How Can You Be Sure God Hears You?

1 Peter 3:12 says – *'the eyes of the Lord are on the righteous, and his ears open to their prayer.'* God hears the prayers of people who

are righteous or perfect. If you know full well that you aren't, don't panic. No-one can make themselves righteous by their own efforts. But the wonderful news is that you can be righteous because of what Jesus has done for you!

Jesus took the punishment for all the things everyone has done, is doing and will do wrong, what the Bible calls sin, when He died on the Cross. God can't pretend sin doesn't matter. But He loves people so much that He doesn't want to punish them, so He punished His Son Jesus instead. This means your sins are forgiven; and when you are born-again, that is you accept Jesus as your Lord and Saviour, that forgiveness becomes real to you. God gives you a new, righteous spirit. This doesn't mean that it's then ok to sin - it isn't - it will lead to many problems in your life and the lives of others, but that sin will not affect your righteous spirit. And it doesn't mean you'll never sin again. But when you do, God wants you to confess it to Him, turn away from it and receive His forgiveness. So does God hear your prayers? If you are born-again, the answer is yes – you are righteous because Jesus died for you and you responded. (To read about being born-again go to page 25)

God's Will

The teaching in this booklet applies to praying for something that is in God's will - something that you know God wants. There are so many things in the Bible about what God wants for people, such as knowing Him, healing, living in love, joy and peace, having their needs met, to name but a few. If you're not sure what God's will is when you're praying for someone, don't just pray a woolly prayer with 'if it's Your will' tagged on the end. Ask God to show you His will and when He does, pray for that.

Free Will

God made people with free will so they can choose how they live. They can accept Jesus or they can reject Him. God didn't make people puppets on strings or pre-programmed robots so He could force them to live His way. God loves you and wants you to love Him back freely. He is always drawing you to Himself in love, but He leaves you free to choose to love Him back or not. That way, when you do, He can have a real love relationship with you, not a forced one. It's the only kind of relationship He wants.

Praying for Others

When you're praying for someone remember they have free will too. This is what makes praying for someone else different from praying for yourself. You have control over your own will, but not over anyone else's. Jesus said in Mark 11:24 – *'whatever you pray and ask for, believe that you have received them, and you shall have them.'* This wonderful principle applies to things that you ask for yourself. It says you have to believe you will receive what you prayed for. As you pray for someone else your part is to believe God will answer, but you can't believe that the person will receive the answer because they may choose to refuse it. In Matthew 23:37 Jesus says to Jerusalem – *'How often I would have gathered your children together, even as a hen gathers her chicks under her wings, and you would not!'* Jesus wanted to love and protect the people of Jerusalem, but they refused to allow Him to do so. God will never override someone's free will. His love for them won't allow Him to do that and He is faithful – He will never go back on the way He designed people to be.

When you pray for someone and nothing changes, it isn't that God didn't hear your prayer or answer it. For instance, say you are praying that the husband of a friend will change his ways and work with his wife to save their marriage. That is a prayer which is pleasing to God and He will answer it and will speak to the husband in his heart about saving his marriage. But if the husband fails to hear because his mind is so occupied with other things, or hears but refuses to respond, God will not force him. Don't think God hasn't heard or answered your prayer and blame Him, when the blame lies with the person's inability to hear what God is saying or his refusal to respond to Him. Each individual is responsible for their own response to God. You can't make it happen for another, but you can pray that it may.

The "May" Principle

New Testament prayers are based on the 'may' principle. Jesus prayed for believers in John 17:21-23 – *'that they may all be one; even as you, Father, are in me, and I in you, that they also may be one in us; that the world may believe that you sent me. The glory which you have given me, I have given to them; that they may be one, even as we are one; I in them, and you in me, that they may be perfected into one; that the world may know that you sent me and loved them, even as you loved me.'* Jesus wants all born-again Christians to be united, or one in Him. But He didn't ask God to make them one; He prayed that they may be one. God has answered that prayer – He has made it possible for believers to live at peace with each other. He has shown them how to do it, but they haven't all responded. Some Christians have used their free will to refuse. Although there are wonderful examples of Christians living and worshipping in peace with each other, the church as a whole has rejected God's answer to Jesus's prayer.

Another example is in Ephesians 3:16-19 where a man called Paul prays for the Christians in Ephesus – *'that he would grant you, according to the riches of his glory, that you may be strengthened with power through his Spirit in the inner person, that Christ may dwell in your hearts through faith, to the end that you, being rooted and grounded in love, may be strengthened to comprehend with all the saints what is the width and length and height and depth, and to know Christ's love which surpasses knowledge, that you may be filled with all the fullness of God. Amen.'* Paul didn't ask God to make these things happen; he asked God to grant the people, or give them, the ability to receive all He had for them. God answered that prayer and the probability is that many of the Ephesian Christians received what God was offering while others failed to recognise what He was doing or refused it and so missed out on God's blessings. Paul prayed that God <u>would give</u> so that they <u>may receive</u>.

To go back to the example of a failing marriage, follow the 'may' principle: don't ask God to make the marriage work, because He's not going to force that on the husband. Instead ask God to guide the husband to think about it and desire it, and pray that he <u>may</u> respond positively. God will answer that prayer. He will make reconciliation possible, and He will draw the husband back to his wife, telling him what will help and what will not. He may hear God's words and respond, or he may not and the marriage fall apart. But if the marriage comes to an end, it doesn't mean God hadn't answered your prayer; He had answered it, but His guidance had been rejected. He will never override free will.

Faith

Faith is so important. God works through people who believe in Him. You don't have to beg God or repeat your prayer over and over –

you can't persuade Him. What you need to do when you pray for someone is to have faith that God will answer. But you can't make the other person have faith to receive that answer, so pray that they <u>may</u> have faith. Ask God, believing He will answer, to send someone along to show them His love. And pray that they <u>may</u> listen to the person He sends and respond in faith.

If you know the person has faith for the answer to the prayer, you can pray together in faith. In <u>Matthew 18:19</u> Jesus says – *'if two of you will agree on earth concerning anything that they will ask, it will be done for them by my Father who is in heaven.'* This is a wonderful promise, but it applies just to the two people praying – it will be done for <u>them</u>, not for someone else.

Is the Person With You?

There's a difference between praying for a person you are with and praying for someone who isn't there. God isn't going to supernaturally 'make' your friend's marriage suddenly work. He will be guiding her husband every step of the way in answer to your prayer, but he has to choose to respond to God.

Now if you are with the husband, you can talk

to him about God's love for him and how He wants to restore his marriage and that He has a plan for him and his wife. You can talk about faith and how he needs to believe that God will answer his prayer. If he responds positively, you can pray for him while you're together asking God for help for the marriage. However, when he leaves you, it is still up to him to believe. You can't make it just happen and God won't make it happen. He loves him too much to override his free will. You can continue to pray in his absence that he may hear God and that he may respond and so save his marriage. God wants to guide him step by step bringing healing to him, his wife and his marriage, but if he won't co-operate God can't do so. He will have answered your prayer, but somewhere along the line the husband has rejected the way God is leading him.

Praying for Someone to be Born-Again

2 Corinthians 4:4 says that the devil — *'has blinded the minds of the unbelieving, that the light of the Good News of the glory of Christ ... should not dawn on them.'* The devil doesn't want people to be born-again; he wants them to keep struggling, trying to get by on their own

instead of with all the power, wisdom and love God has for them. So he has blinded their minds - the world is full of people who just won't consider Jesus or who will go to great lengths to 'disprove' Him. But Jesus has defeated the devil on the Cross and as a born-again believer you have His authority. So use it - bind the spiritual blindness on the person in the name of Jesus that they <u>may</u> be free to receive His Good News. Then pray that God will send someone along to tell them about Jesus, and that they <u>may</u> be open to listen to what that person says and respond.

Praying for Healing for Others

Jesus made it very clear that faith is needed for healing, so you can't just command healing in Jesus's name for someone who isn't with you and expect results. There has to be faith operating from their side. On just a few occasions, Jesus healed someone who wasn't with Him but in each case, someone very close to the sick person had come to Him on their behalf in faith. He responded to the faith of that person rather than that of the sick person, but faith was still operating on the side of the sick person.

So the very first thing to pray for someone who needs healing and isn't with you is that God will reveal His love to them and His desire for them to be well and that the person <u>may</u> hear what He's saying and respond. Ask God to send someone to them who will explain it to them and pray that the person <u>may</u> be willing to hear and respond and reach out in faith for their healing.

There was just one time when Jesus couldn't heal many people. It was in His home town where the people who had known Him from a child wouldn't believe He was the Son of God and so had no faith in Him. <u>Mark 6:5-6</u> says — *'He could do no mighty work there, except that he laid his hands on a few sick people, and healed them. He marveled because of their unbelief.'* So you can't command healing unless you know the person has faith in Jesus for it. But if you spend time with them and explain how Jesus has won their healing for them on the Cross, their faith might rise so you can command healing in Jesus's name.

(For more detail on healing, read the booklet 'God Wants You to Be Well'.)

Pray for Others

It's such a privilege to pray for other people, knowing it's what God wants you to do and that He will answer as you pray in faith. Pray for others what you believe He wants for them, and pray that they <u>may</u> hear His voice and respond to it. God will do everything He can, without force, to bring that person to receive what you've prayed for them. Exciting? Definitely!

2

Praying for Yourself

Do you ask God for things, but feel He doesn't hear or doesn't answer? Or do you feel you don't deserve anything from God or that He doesn't care?

Does God Hear Your Prayers?

<u>1 Peter 3:12</u> says – *'the eyes of the Lord are on the righteous, and his ears open to their prayer.'* God hears the prayers of righteous or perfect people. If you're thinking, "Well that eliminates me!" don't worry. No-one can make themselves righteous by their own efforts. But

Praying for Yourself

anyone can be righteous, not because of what they do, but because of what Jesus has done!
Sin is what the Bible calls the things everyone has done, is doing and will do wrong. God can't ignore sin – He is just and it has to be punished. But He loves people so much, so instead of punishing them He punished His Son Jesus. Jesus took the punishment for all sin when He died on the Cross. Your sins are forgiven; and when you accept Jesus as your Lord and Saviour and are born-again, that forgiveness becomes real. And God gives you a brand new, righteous spirit.

This doesn't mean it's ok to sin – it will lead to lots of problems in your life and the lives of others, but it will not affect your righteous spirit. And it doesn't mean you'll never sin again. When you do, confess it to God, turn away from it and receive forgiveness. So God does hear your prayers if you're born-again – you are righteous because Jesus died for you and you responded.

It doesn't mean that if you're not born-again God will never hear you, but it's not until you are born-again that you have the promise that He hears your prayers. (To read about being born-again go to page 25)

Praying for Yourself

Praying is about so much more than asking God for things. As you grow in your relationship with Him and realise more and more just how much He loves you, you'll find you spend less time asking Him for things and more time simply loving Him and praising and thanking Him. But sometimes you do need something or you need guidance or wisdom and God wants you to ask Him for it. How do you go about it?

God's Will

This booklet is about praying for something that is God's will – something that He wants for you. If you don't know what His will is in a particular situation, ask Him to show you and when He does, pray for that. Don't pray a woolly prayer and tag 'if it's your will' on the end.

When Jesus was praying before His death He said in Luke 22:42 – *'Father, if you are willing, remove this cup from me. Nevertheless, not my will, but yours, be done.'* He was struggling with knowing that He was going to be tortured and killed, carrying the weight of all sin and sickness. But what He said wasn't a woolly prayer. He knew exactly what God's will was, and having expressed His struggle, He said He'd do it God's way.

The Desires of Your Heart

Psalm 37:4 says – *'delight yourself in the LORD, and he will give you the desires of your heart.'* This doesn't mean that God will give you anything you want whether it's good for you or not. James 4:3 says – *'You ask, and don't receive, because you ask with wrong motives, so that you may spend it on your pleasures.'* Your motives are important. God isn't going to fund a wrong or self-centred life style. He won't give you something which you want only to prove yourself better than someone else or to fritter away doing wrong things or on things of no value. But as you delight in God - look to Him for your needs and enjoy your love relationship with Him, He will give you new desires that match His desires for you.

God the Giver

Philippians 4:19 says – *'My God will supply every need of yours.'* When you ask God for something, ask confidently, knowing that He wants to give. But even more than that - God is generous. He wants to give and give and give. Jesus said in John 10:10 – *'I came that they may have life, and may have it abundantly.'* That's what Jesus wants for you – abundant life! As you ask for things that are in God's will you can be sure He will give and delight to do so.

Jesus told His followers to ask and it would be given them. He explained that if human parents will want to give good things to their children, how much more will God – your heavenly Father. He illustrated it with a story in Luke 11:5-8 – *'if you go to a friend at midnight, and tell him, 'Friend, lend me three loaves of bread, for a friend of mine has come to me from a journey, and I have nothing to set before him,' and he from within will answer and say, 'Don't bother me. The door is now shut, and my children are with me in bed. I can't get up and give it to you'? I tell you, although he will not rise and give it to him because he is his friend, yet because of his persistence, he will get up and give him as many as he needs.'* Jesus wasn't saying God was like this friend who was annoyed at being disturbed and reluctant to help. He was saying that if even a person like that eventually gave what was needed, how much more would God give willingly and freely.

Put God First

Matthew 6:31-33 says – *'don't be anxious, saying, 'What will we eat?', 'What will we drink?' or, 'With what will we be clothed?' ... for your heavenly Father knows that you need all these things. But seek first God's Kingdom, and his righteousness; and all these things will be given to you as well.'* God has promised to give you all you need for daily living. It doesn't mean that you can't have the enjoyment of deciding what to wear and planning meals. It means you don't need to worry about these things. If you put God first and seek to live the way He wants you to, He will make sure you have enough of all the necessities. He looks at the heart, and if you are loving Him, He will respond.

Ask in Faith

It is important to have faith when you pray. In Mark 11:24 Jesus said – *'all things whatever you pray and ask for, believe that you have received them, and you shall have them.'* When you've asked God for something, you don't need to keep asking Him. Jesus said to believe for what you pray for. If this doesn't seem to work for you, it isn't Jesus's promise that is faulty; it's your lack of faith. That sounds harsh I know, but I say it to help you. It takes effort – you have to decide to believe and refuse to doubt. It's not easy, but try it – choose to have faith, refuse to think any other way and see the results. Thank Him that He's heard and that what you've asked for is coming and wait in faith.

Believe You Will Receive God's Wisdom

<u>James 1:5-8</u> says – *'if any of you lacks wisdom, let him ask of God, who gives to all liberally and without reproach, and it will be given to him. But let him ask in faith, without any doubting, for he who doubts is like a wave of the sea, driven by the wind and tossed. For let that man shouldn't think that he will receive anything from the Lord. He is a double-minded man, unstable in all his ways.'*

If you don't know what to do in any situation ask God for wisdom and guidance. God gives it 'without reproach'. That means without judging you to see if you deserve it. He gives it freely to those who ask as long as they ask believing that He will give the answer.

When you don't know what to do in a particular situation, you can so easily be anxious, imagining lots of different scenarios and outcomes – it really is like being tossed around in the sea in a storm. When you've asked God, decide to believe He <u>will</u> show you what to do and wait for the answer in peace. Make an effort to stop your thoughts running away with you. If they start to do so, stop and thank God that He is going to give you His wisdom. The wisdom may come from reading the Bible or through another person, or a particular way forward may settle in your mind. If you feel at peace about this you can know that it is God's answer and put it into action confidently.

Be Specific

In <u>Matthew 6:8</u> Jesus says – *'your Father knows what things you need, before you ask him.'* There is a wonderful comfort in the fact that God knows exactly what you need and longs to give it to you. But He does want you to ask. He wants you to understand that it is only through Him that your needs can be fully met. <u>James 4:2</u> says – *'You don't have, because you don't ask.'* God wants you to ask specifically for what you need. He longs to give you good things. Don't limit Him by only wanting the cheapest or the minimum. Give Him the opportunity to bless you. But remember to check your motives.

In <u>Matthew 6:7</u> Jesus says — *'In praying, don't use vain repetitions, as the Gentiles do; for they think that they will be heard for their much speaking.'* God wants you to ask simply, directly and specifically. There are many religions where you are expected to perform rituals or repeat chants. God simply wants you to ask Him with an open child-like heart that believes He will provide for you, and thank Him even before the answer comes.

A Delayed Answer

In <u>Daniel 9:21-23</u> a man called Daniel explains — *'While I was speaking in prayer, … Gabriel … being caused to fly swiftly … talked with me, and said, "Daniel … At the beginning of your petitions the commandment went out, and I have come to tell you."'* God answered Daniel's prayer by sending the angel Gabriel to him while he was still praying.

But in <u>Daniel 10:12-13</u> he says that the angel came in answer to one of his prayers three weeks after he had prayed it. When he did come the angel said — *'from the first day that you set your heart to understand, and to humble yourself before your God, your words were heard. I have come for your words' sake. But the prince of the kingdom of Persia withstood me twenty-one days; but, behold, Michael, one of the chief princes, came to help me.'* To Daniel it must have seemed as if God hadn't answered this later prayer. But the angel explained that the reason for the delay wasn't that God hadn't answered Daniel's prayer, but that the devil had tried to stop the answer getting to him. The devil didn't succeed, but he managed to delay it.

If God doesn't seem to be answering your prayer, don't give up or blame Him. He has answered and it will come.

Your Healing

Jesus said to speak to sickness. Don't talk to God about it, asking Him to heal you – He's already won your healing through Jesus's suffering and death. Instead, talk to the sickness about God and command it to go in Jesus's name. There is a lot more about this in the booklet 'God Wants You to Be Well'.

The Prayer of Agreement

In Matthew 18:19 Jesus says – *'if two of you will agree on earth concerning anything that they will ask, it will be done for them by my Father who is in heaven.'* This is a wonderful promise. If you pray with someone else for something for yourself, and you agree together that it is God's will, you have Jesus's promise that it will come. If you start to doubt, turn your thoughts around –thank God for His promise and thank Him for the answer to your prayer even before it comes.

In the Name of Jesus

In John 16:23-24 Jesus told His followers – *'whatever you may ask of the Father in my name, he will give it to you. Until now, you have asked nothing in my name. Ask, and you will receive, that your joy may be made full.'* This is why Christians often end their prayers with 'in Jesus name'. While He was on the earth, His followers asked Him for what they needed, and Jesus asked God for them. Now Jesus was saying that they should ask God directly in His name. That's how to pray today. Take Jesus at His word - pray in His name and believe for the answer.

Pray for Yourself

Put God first in your life, choosing His way of looking at things and doing things, and He will give you all you need. When you do ask, believe that He will answer your prayer, thank Him and wait in faith. It's such freedom to realise that you don't need to nag God or try to persuade Him. He is infinitely generous and is longing to give you all you need and more besides. Follow Him and believe Him and start to experience abundant life.

Being Born-Again

When you acknowledge Jesus as God and decide to follow Him, you make Him your Lord. When you accept His sacrifice on the Cross for yourself personally, you make Him your Saviour. You are then born-again and have a new perfect spirit. God becomes your Father and you His child, and you can start to enjoy your personal love relationship with Him.

Romans 10:9 says – *'If you will confess with your mouth that Jesus is Lord, and believe in your heart that God raised him from the dead, you will be saved.'* Tell God you are sorry for the wrong things you do, say and think. Choose to believe that Jesus is Lord, that He died for you and is now alive. Accept Him as your Lord and Saviour. Say it with your voice and believe it in your heart.

If you've done that sincerely, you are now born-again and Jesus has come to live in you. Everything you've ever done wrong or ever will do wrong is forgiven, and after this life is over, you'll live in peace and joy with your loving Father God for ever.

As a child of God, you now have a whole new family of brothers and sisters. Tell a trusted Christian that you are now born-again so they can help you in your new life in Jesus. And you have the Bible to help you understand and experience more of God's love for you and all Jesus has done and won for you. It will help you to live your life in the best possible way – His way.

Life in Jesus

Katherine Hilditch has been teaching in local churches for many years. She also trained a church ministry team which she set up and led with her husband for 17 years. Her first booklet, which she wrote in 2013, encouraged many people so she started to write more and then created her website to make them available to everyone. They are all completely free to read online or download and print out and there is no limit to the number of booklets you may print. To read her story and find all the booklets go to –

LifeinJesus.net

Titles include –

Spirit, Soul and Body
Praying for Others
God Loves You
Who is the Holy Spirit?
God Wants You to Be Well
Praying for Yourself
God's Not Angry With You
Prosperity?
Be Transformed
Forgiveness

Printed in Great Britain
by Amazon